Notice

Briana Gibson

Presentation by *BookLeaf Publishing*

Web: www.bookleafpub.com

E-mail: info@bookleafpub.com

ISBN: 9789358310320

First edition 2023

Home

The solid earth under my feet
Grass between my bare toes
And earth's energy running through me
Cleansing me,
Grounding me.
The crunch of leaves under my feet
As I walk through the woods
And the smell of decaying leaves
And plant matter returning to
Nourish the soil and
Bring new life.
The feel of the tree's rough bark
Under my fingers.
The smell of earth before it rains.

Rain on my face,
Pounding on the roof,
Splashing onto my legs and arms
As I jump into a puddle.
Water running over my bare body
As I stand in the shower,
Thankful for clear running water
To cleanse my mind, body and spirit.
My body gliding through the water,
Pool, lake or ocean

Completely submerged,
Weightless and free.
The trickle of a stream,
Meandering through the woods.
The roar, or drip, of a waterfall,
Waves pounding the shore,
Ocean or lake expanding before my eyes,
Seemingly endless,
Reflecting the bright sun...

Sunlight on water.
It's warmth on my face.
I close my eyes and feel into it more
Warming, charging my whole self.
The gradual growing glow
As the sun rises in the early morning,
And the warm, rich colors
As it fades behind the earth at night.
Warm concrete beneath my feet,
Sometimes comforting,
Sometimes painful,
Too hot to handle.
Flames crackling in a fire,
The smell of burning wood.
It permeates my clothes, my hair.
The fire's heat warming my hands, my body.
Comforting at a distance,
Burning if I get too close
Or linger too long.

I feed it ideas, memories and patterns
That I'm ready to get rid of.
It's heat transforms them into ash,
Now ready to fertilize the firmament
And grow into something new.

The wind picks up the ash,
Deposits it where it sees fit.
I can't see the wind, the air,
But I sense evidence of it
All around me.
I see things spinning, whirling, twirling,
Flying, seemingly on their own.
I hear the wind playing with the trees,
Rustling their leaves
Sometimes right above me,
Sometimes further away.
A dance I'm delighted to witness.
The wind plays with other things too...
The eaves of my house
The wind chime hanging by the door.
And me
Sometimes as a soft caress
Sometimes whipping through my hair.

How thankful I am for all these
Earthly experiences.
Earth, Water, Fire and Air
I pray for the Presence

To revel in them everyday.
For how easily it is to
Go about our days
And miss these gifts,
Unique to this life on earth,
Presented to us each and every day
In so many ways.

All we have to do is
Notice.

A Tear Escapes

A tear escapes,
Runs down my cheek.

I'm not crying.
My eyes are watering.
I have allergies.

Even as I type those words
I believe them
In my brain
I've said them so many times
Like a lie that you tell
Over and over
So much so that
It becomes truth.

Even my body believes those words.
I feel no emotion
As that tear streams down my face.
Just watery eyes.
Just a tear.
Nothing else.

Ahh, but I've begun listening to my heart again.

And my heart whispers another idea…
What if that tear is not just a tear?
What if that tear is an
Escaped emotion
That has never been allowed to be felt?

Words I've heard,
Words I've said
Start popping up…

Don't cry.
Don't laugh.
Not too hard anyway.
Don't dance.
You don't know how to do it right.
You'll look ridiculous if you do.
Don't sing.
You can't.
Not as good as her anyway.
Not too loud.
Not too much.
Shhhh.

If you stay quiet you won't be noticed,
Won't be made fun of…
Won't be judged…
Won't upset them.

And so over the years

I trained myself not to feel,
At least not to feel too much,
In order to survive;
To survive a world full of people
Who are uncomfortable with
Big emotions.
People who have also been told
Don't cry.
Don't be too much.

Slowly I'm learning to
Feel those feelings again.
It's oh so important.
Important not only for
My health,
My happiness.
But for the health and happiness
Of the world.

And so I notice...
I notice those sensations in my body...
The tightness in my chest
The pain in my belly
My clenched fists
My pulled up shoulders.

And then I explore a little more
To see what emotion
Is behind the sensation.

I talk to that emotion.
I name it, acknowledge it.
I empathize with it.
I allow it.
Even the "negative" ones.
Fear, anger, jealousy
They are emotions too.
They deserve acknowledgement
Just as much as all the rest.

But it's a slow process

Kind of like training the body
To run or swim.
I know the motions.
But as much as I know what to do and
Want to do it perfectly every time
This takes practice too.

And so when the occasional tear
Slips down my cheek
I won't dismiss it any longer.
I will give it a nod of acknowledgement,
A smile of gratitude, and
Wipe it away with a blessing and
A prayer that next time I can do the same
For the emotion that escaped inside it.

Grief

The anger has dissipated
More and more.
Once again I'm allowing
My heart to open,
Ever so slightly,
Dipping in my toe..
How does it feel?
I can only allow it
To open so much,
To feel so much.
The slight opening
Allows in the grief anew.

It's a softer grief, now.
Tears fill my eyes,
My chest aches.
But I feel it, acknowledge it,
Say a little thank you to myself,
Knowing that this process is
Moving me forward.

I continue with the day to day,
One foot in front of the other,
More acutely aware of all things around me
That I am thankful for...

The pitter patter of toddler feet exploring all the
nooks and crannies of our
Sweet and cozy home,
A fridge full of food,
The crazy antics of my middle children as
They pop in and out of the room,
And the silent company of my teenager,
As we sit together on the couch.

The opening of my heart
Allows me to feel
The gratitude
The joy
The pleasure
All the more deeply.
But also the pain,
The grief.
Sometimes it's more than
I can bare.

So, slowly, slowly,
My love,
Take your time.
Be gentle with yourself.

It's all there,
Waiting to be experienced
And felt

By you, as deeply as you choose,
When and as you are ready.

Divine Truth

There is a Divine Truth that
Runs much deeper than
Our minds can
Conceptualize or objectify.

This Divine Truth
Can be only perceived
In stillness,
In beauty,
In nature,
In the feelings so intense
That they could crush us
Or reveal the
Entirety of all the universe,
Hidden deep within each of our
Hearts and souls.

It is a knowing
Beyond definition
Beyond words
Beyond thought
That can only be perceived
By each of us
As we connect to that
Which is both
Within and beyond us.

The Void

Ah, the feelings
And sensations
That come with this
Human experience.

Grief,
Agony,
Joy,
Pain,
Relief,
Pleasure,
Loneliness.

To feel all of it
So deeply is
Mind-blowing
And soul crushing,
Ecstasy
And agony.

How can one person
Handle it all,
Experience it all,
Without numbing it down
Or losing their mind?

The Void

I see the feelings,
Acknowledge them.
I feel into them.

It feels like
Trying to be strong
On the outside,
When you just want to crumble
On the inside.
It's being so turned on by life
And no one to share it with
At the depths you want to go.

But it's all there for a reason.
Don't try to make it go away.
Be with it for a little bit longer.
For as long as it takes.

And when it feels like
Too much,
Take all this with you, into
The Void.

The Void.
No time
No place

No sounds
No sights
No words

Nothing to do
Nothing to fix
No one to be

Relax into this

Stay as long as you want.

Feel the Void
Envelope you
Nourish you
Comfort and
Support you.

Loneliness

Driving home.

Feeling into the loneliness

Accented by having just been with people, And
by the desire to be with people again.

Certain people in this case.

People who help me feel more deeply connected

Connected to Myself
Connected to God
Connected to All

Obsession, Addiction

Sometimes the longings feel that strong.

I breech other people's boundaries,
If only with my thoughts

Just for the opportunity to feel connected
through all avenues.
Emotional, Physical, Spiritual

I wonder if I will every find a person who
fulfills all of those at once.

Just the thought of the possibility of
That person coming into my life
Quickens my heart

But I can say honestly that I am not
Attached to having this.

I long for it
But I have so much gratitude for
Everything I have in my life
And all the beautiful people who
Bring so much to me

But still the loneliness tugs

I see it
I feel it
I allow it
I honor it

Thank you beautiful loneliness.

Christ

He is already here.
He is alive
In each one of us.
We all have the ability to
Live through him.
We're not waiting for a
Physical savior to return.
The world is waiting for
Each of us to bring forth the
Living Christ in us.

Many Stories

A black crow flies
In front of my car from
Left to right
Followed closely by
Two smaller birds.
They weave and
Chase and avert.
I wonder what the story is.

So many stories exist
Just on the peripheral
Of our own lives.

Not only stories of other people
But all the other creatures
Who share this earth with us,
Each with stories of their own.

My Beloved

My body craves you,
To be touched by you,
Embraced by you,
Explored and discovered by you.

My fingers long to touch you
To explore every inch of you,
To elicit sweet pleasure in you,
To caress and comfort and hold you.

My soul craves you
To be seen by you,
Acknowledged by you,
Embraced and remembered by you.

My spirit longs to delve into yours,
To lay you bare,
To remind you of your divinity,
To remind you of my divinity,
To help you remember all the times
We've been together before,
To exalt in our Union,
Once again.

Stolen Moments

Stolen moments…
Between work and kids and
All the other responsibilities
Of Real Life

Real Life?
Is the daily grind of
Work and responsibilities
Real Life?
Or are the stolen moments of
Bliss
Real Life?
Maybe it is both
The sweet balance of the two.
Can I find bliss
In all I do?

Stolen moments
Three hours here
An overnight there
Stolen moments where
It is just the two of us
Each only existing as the other perceives
Perfectly open hearted, caring,
Compassionate, tender.

Stolen moments of touching,
Skin to skin,
Fingers exploring, caressing,
Bodies intertwined,
Gazing into each other's eyes,
Deep, dreaming conversations,
Being cracked open, explored,
Moments of ecstatic bliss.

Moments of ecstatic bliss,
Made even more poignant
By the knowledge that, for now,
Our time together is fleeting…

Ecstatic bliss slowly transforms into
Sweet agony
The sweet agony of knowing
That our time together is
Quickly coming to an end,
At least for today.

I remember.
I remember now,
The sweet agony of
Separating from Source
A necessity to know
The ecstatic bliss of Union.

Alarm sounds
Noooo
I'm not ready to leave this
Just a few more
Stolen moments
Before I have to walk out the door.
Again.

It feels like a literal
Tearing away,
Heavy.
I really don't want to go.
Tears threaten at
The back of my throat
And the corners of my eyes.
It gets harder and harder
Every time.
When will there be
No more separation?

And yet…
What happens when
There is more
Union and togetherness
Than separation?
Do we forget
The ecstatic bliss of
Being together
In stolen moments?

Is that the fear?
How do we hold onto
Or continue to find
The ecstatic bliss
Without the sweet agony of
Separation?

I don't have an answer.
I'm learning that I don't have to.
I connect to the bliss of,
Or is it the sweet agony of
Not knowing.

All I can do,
All I need to do
Is rest in each
Stolen, conscious moment,
Feeling, embracing, loving, even,
All the feelings that come.
Trusting in the unveiling
And in the plan that is
Slowly bringing us
Back to Union,
Where the stolen moments are
Merely moments, and
We are one.

Agony

There is something
So sweet,
So divine,
So alive
In feeling agony.

In loving something so much
That the taking away of,
Or even just the thought of that
Feels like having
Your soul ripped out.

The agony of separation…
A stark contrast to the
Bliss of Union.

Will agony always
Be necessary
In order to experience the
Bliss of Union?

Worry

Worry.

The little gnawing voices
At the edge of consciousness
Sometimes so quiet,
It's barely perceptible.
Sometimes so loud
It's hard to focus on
Anything else.

Worry.

Stuck

Stuck in a perpetual loop…
Worry, worry
How am I going to make ends meet?
Am I doing enough?
Am I good enough?
Am I enough?
Why can't I be enough?

Then I remember to
Tap into the eternal Love…
I am love.
I am exactly where I need to be.
Look for joy in every moment.
Practice Gratitude.
This is an abundant world,
More than enough for everyone.
I feel free, connected, held, supported.

But those feelings don't pay the bills
Or support relationships,
Or raise kids,
Or run a business.
Or do they?
Regardless,
Those things require action.

Then take action,
Heart-centered action.
It sounds so simple.
Pick us up by the bootstraps,
Nose to the grindstone.
I know what I need to do.
Just do it.

It works for a day or two,
A week if I'm lucky, maybe two.
But life happens…
And I'm supposed to handle
All life's little emergencies,
A clogged toilet here,
The toddler dumps glue on the floor there,
Pre-teen can't sleep,
Teen needs to be heard and witnessed,
Wait, what about the 9 year old?

Handle all of it
With grace and joy and gratitude,
And pay the bills,
Make and keep the appointments,
Maintain relationships,
Be a good friend, partner, sister, daughter,
Build your business,
Support your partners,
Teach Love.

But how do I teach love
When I'm being so unloving to myself.
Oh yeah,
Practice self love, self care,
Feel your emotions,
Love the one who feels your emotions,
Connect to your higher power,
Don't forget to meditate,
Yoga, run…

The list is endless
How can one person maintain?
But you must,
It's what you're here for…
To show people a different way.

So, connect
Gratitude,
Joy,
Trust,
Surrender.

It works, again,
For awhile.
It is a practice,
I tell myself,
I tell others…
It's a spiral,

It's getting easier,
I'm learning more,
I'm growing.
It won't always feel like this.

But how much longer can I hold on,
Be strong?
Find gratitude?
Surrender more?

Let it all fall apart?

But who will be there to pick up the pieces?
Who will catch me when I fall?

I'm in Love with Your Soul

I'm in love with your soul.
With your eyes and body and mind, yes.
But I'm in love with your soul.
I don't know that I have ever experienced
another person at the depths that I have
experienced you.
I see now why people talk about
soul mates or the other half of my soul.
You are what has been missing from my life,
what my soul has been longing for.
But yet, I had to be complete in myself to have
found you.
Ha. The crazy paradox that is this life.

Drowning

I feel like I'm drowning
Struggling to keep my head above water
So tired of trying to keep afloat

He is a life preserver,
But hard to hold onto.
The waves of reality come crashing
I lose my grip and
Am plummeted back into the depths

I work to break the surface
To catch a breath,
And he is there for me
A place to rest.

But I can't stay there long
Not yet,
The waves are too many
And I am knocked down again.
And again I wonder if I have the strength to
Keep swimming,
To break the surface
For the thousandth time.
Sometimes it seems like it would be
Easier to give up, stop struggling

And let the water take me.

I Am Her

It dawned on me tonight

I am Her.

I am the woman I've always longed to be.
Is this what your 40's feel like?
Or is it all the work I've done
Looking at myself and
Refusing to compromise who I am any more,
Making decisions based on what is best for me
and my children,
What makes me feel good,
What is good for me,
What makes my heart sing?
Maybe it's both.

I am Her.

I am the woman who
Dances and sings in her kitchen,
Walks barefoot outside,
Does cartwheels in her yard.

I am the woman who
Lives by her own schedule,

Her own set of rules.

My kids run wild,
Play,
Learn what and when they want to learn,
Rest when they feel like resting.
I learn from them.

I am the woman who
Has freedom in her movement,
Feels good in her body,
Relishes in the little things…

The sound of my children's laughter,
The sight of the clouds in the sky,
The feel of soft dewy grass under my feet,
The touch of my lover's hand on my skin,
The smell of lilacs wafting in the air.

I am Her.

I am the woman who is
Reminiscent of the child she used to be,
Only with more experience and knowledge,
More ability to move gracefully through it all,
Who moves with abandon,
Not thinking or caring about who might be
watching or what they are thinking
Who takes joy in merely being alive and

All the experiences that encompasses,
Who sees the potential and magic in everything.

I am Her.

Outside Looking In

I'm outside looking in…

Sometimes I'm in,
Experiencing and feeling everything,
Present.
Deep feelings.
Not judging,
Just accepting and
Loving the experience of all.

But sometimes I'm outside
Looking in.
Seeing myself experiencing everything.

But when you're watching the one experiencing,
You are no longer experiencing.

I judge,
I label,
I analyze,
I try to predict
And plan
And prevent
And protect.
I try to control.

It feels good to
Analyze, to
Categorize.
It feels
Safe,
Predictable.

Its where I've spent
Most of my life—
In order to numb out the
Intense feelings.

The rest of the world
Isn't comfortable witnessing
Intense feelings.
I feel their discomfort.
Intense feelings are not controllable
They are not productive,
At least from a consumerism perspective,
They expose the truth.
They are the the truth.

But to be the experiencer,
In,
That goes beyond
Just feeling good.
It's bliss.
To be in the moment,

Present,
To fully feel each moment…
The "good,"
Joy, fun, elation, glee, thrill, beauty
As well as the "bad,"
Pain, anger, agony, loneliness, hurt.
Bliss.
It's bliss to be able to
Experience those things,
To feel it all.

And to think,
That only here on Earth,
As a human being,
Can these depths of feelings
Be felt.

But it takes
An endurance,
A tolerance,
To feel so intensely.

Most of us have lived a
Large portion of our lives
Numbed out,
Maybe even judging
The ones who can't or won't
Live that way.

Stepping back into
Fully feeling all the things
Is intense.
It can be a lot,
Too much
To handle all at once.

So, slowly, slowly,
My love,
Dip your toe
Back into feeling again,
Like you did when you were a child,
Before the world taught you
Not to feel.

The Sweetest Sleep

Sometime around 3 am I became conscious that
we had been in some sort of embrace since we
drifted off to sleep together…

Held, Caressed, Loved
All night.

How I have longed for this my entire life.

"I came in praying for you."
The lyrics return to me again.
Over and over I am reminded of how true They
are for me, for him.
A million little reminders, day after day
Of how I have longed for exactly
Who he is and
What we are together.

In this early morning,
Realizing that I have spent most of the night
Being held and touched
By someone who loves me and
Whom I love and adore.
My heart swells,
Threatening to burst out of my chest,

And I am filled with overwhelming gratitude.

Realizing that it is the first time,
I thank God for bringing him into my life.

Wow. Why is this the first time I have
Expressed my gratitude for him in this way?
My tendency is to berate myself for
Neglecting to do so before this,
But being loved so purely and tenderly
By someone,
Allows me to love myself in the same way…
And I realize that up until now
I wasn't sure this was real and
That I wasn't going to get hurt again,
That I wasn't deluding myself into
Seeing something that wasn't really there.
I give myself grace and compassion
For not doing what I wasn't ready to do.

I told him I loved him early on,
Even if my hurt and wounding
Couldn't believe it,
My heart and soul recognized it.

He has shown me over and over again
That I can trust him
That he loves me
That he will be here for me

That I am safe to show him the
Parts of me that I, myself,
Haven't been able to fully accept.
He accepts them.
He won't turn away from them when they are
even too much for me.
He loves me.

I don't know why
This sweetest sleep
Is the trigger that opens
My eyes and
My heart to
Help me see into the depths of
All that God has given me in him.
It feels like one of those signs
Your soul leaves for you on your journey,
To help you remember
That It's there
That God's there.
Especially in those times where
It seems darkest and
You're not sure you can go on,
God is there.
And look at this beautiful gift
God has given you
To help carry you through
And beyond into the light
That is your future together.

Like a flower slowly blooming
(Oh, God, I know where the cheesy lines and
Lyrics I used to scoff at come from)
The way he loves me has
Allowed me to open to receive
All that is being given to me.
And how beautiful,
That here in the dark,
In and out of consciousness,
In this sweetest sleep,
I see it all clearly for the first time…

Thank you for him.

Holding Space

Silence from him.
And then his truth.
How could these things
Possibly fit into his
Vision of the future?
Ah, I know that feeling well.

So I listen.
I acknowledge.
I hold space.
I hold space for his words,
His emotions,
His reality.
And I hold space for the possibility
All the possibilities
That what I feel might not come to be.
There is free will.
And there are infinite
Timelines and possibilities.
And I know that whatever timeline this
Conscious version of myself follows,
I want to follow it with this man,
For as long as it works for the both of us.
I love him so deeply that
I can't even explain.

It's that same knowing of
Truth and love that
Words just can't do justice to.

When I acknowledge
How much I love him,
It scares me,
My ego,
The little "i,"
The little girl inside me
Who is afraid to get hurt again,
Afraid that this love is an illusion.
And he echoes my fears
When he moves on and
Starts to talk about trust and
How even though he trusts me,
He will never truly trust again.

And my heart breaks.
Not in the way a
Starry-eyed, 20 something
Version of me's heart
Would have broken
At dashed hopes,
But it breaks for him.
And it breaks for the part of me
Who relates to all he says.
It breaks for our innocence and
The wounded parts of us.

But I know that through this wounding
And the healing
That has and is following,
That something beautiful is
Transpiring, transforming.

For me, I am free to feel again.
Because I have experienced
Some of my worst fears,
Some of the deepest hurts
I didn't know were possible,
I am left raw and open, and
I feel again,
Much like I felt everything
When I was a little girl,
Before I learned to close everything off
For the comfort of those around me.

And so, as my heart breaks
For the both of us,
I am able to feel the beauty of
Feeling all of it and
Acknowledge how it has
Brought me, and us
To this moment and
A love and
A caring and
A tenderness that

I always wanted but
Never believed existed.

And so I hold space.
I hold space for
All that we're going through and
All that we've been through.
And I hold space for
Whatever will come.

There is peace in not needing
Things to be one way or another,
Not needing to control
What happens or
How he or I feel.
There is peace in letting go.
There is peace in acceptance.

Tender Little Moments

It seems to me
In all the little moments
That I have never been
Touched, held, caressed,
Cared for before,
Until now.

Surrender, submit…
Words that I have fought against
For most of my life.
Now, in your arms, your care,
I do so eagerly, readily.
And when I do,
I crave it more and more,
Deeper and deeper,
Until we are one.

Through you,
I can feel the love of God.
Is that wrong? Sacrilege?
How can it be?
Maybe that is part of why we are here,
Together, manifest as humans,
To show and experience together
The love of God,

Manifest into form.

Too deep? Maybe.
So I swing back and forth
Between surrendering to you,
To the moment
And trying to understand
The secrets of the Universe.
You connect me to it all.
And now back again,
To surrender into your embrace,
Held, loved by it all.

Receiving

"You're so open,"
She tells me,
Time and time again.

How to find the balance
Between remaining open
To all this life has to give,
To all the guidance available,
To divine love,
To all there is to be experienced,
To all the souls
Needing to be seen
To be witnessed,
And not being dashed apart
On the rocks of
Other people's unconsciousness,
Not being used up,
Drained until I am a shell,
Not being so immersed in
Someone else that
I lose who I am.

Mary was told to put away her
Shield of Protection.
Am I called to do the same?

I came in with no shield,
Completely open.
But, ooo, this world can feel harsh
When you're so wide open to it.
So I quickly learned to
Put up my shield.

Then life dashed my shield apart.
Thankfully my faith and
The ability to lean into
God's love,
Allowed me to not
Put it back up so quickly
To remember the beauty of
Living so openly.

For being open means
You are open to feel
All the Love and Truth and Beauty
That is always flowing
Towards us, through us,
If only you are open to see it.
Messages, interactions, lessons
Feel differently when you're
Open to feeling the love
Available to you at all times.

It's the same message of

This noticing…
Slowly, slowly,
My love,
Take your time.
Feel what you can feel,
Open to what you can,
Stay balanced and grounded
In who you are,
In your vibration,
Put up your shield
When it all feels like too much,
Take refuge in The Void,
But only stay as long as you need,
For there is so much to
Be felt and experienced,

If only we're open
To receive.

9 789358 310320